Mouhamadou Bamba Mboup

How can I earn $1,000 a day online?

AF535300

Mouhamadou Bamba Mboup

How can I earn $1,000 a day online?

ScienciaScripts

Imprint
Any brand names and product names mentioned in this book are subject to trademark, brand or patent protection and are trademarks or registered trademarks of their respective holders. The use of brand names, product names, common names, trade names, product descriptions etc. even without a particular marking in this work is in no way to be construed to mean that such names may be regarded as unrestricted in respect of trademark and brand protection legislation and could thus be used by anyone.

Cover image: www.ingimage.com

This book is a translation from the original published under ISBN 978-620-6-71928-1.

Publisher:
Sciencia Scripts
is a trademark of
Dodo Books Indian Ocean Ltd. and OmniScriptum S.R.L publishing group

120 High Road, East Finchley, London, N2 9ED, United Kingdom
Str. Armeneasca 28/1, office 1, Chisinau MD-2012, Republic of Moldova, Europe
Printed at: see last page
ISBN: 978-620-7-98655-2

Copyright © Mouhamadou Bamba Mboup
Copyright © 2024 Dodo Books Indian Ocean Ltd. and OmniScriptum S.R.L publishing group

HOW CAN I MAKE $1,000 A DAY ON THE INTERNET?

MOUHAMADOU BAMBA MBOUP

CONTENTS

1. INTRODUCTION TO ONLINE REVENUE GENERATION

The advantages of earning money on the internet

Earning money online has a number of advantages that are attracting more and more people to explore this path. Here are some of the main advantages:

Flexibility: One of the main advantages is the flexibility offered by working online. You can work anytime, anywhere, making it easy to balance your professional and personal life.

Low initial costs: Unlike traditional businesses, starting up online often requires minimal investment. You can start with little or no money and gradually build up your business.

Large target audience: the Internet offers worldwide access to a large audience, which means that your revenue opportunities are not limited by your geographical location. You can reach customers all over the world.

Diversity of income sources: On the internet, there are a multitude of ways to earn money, whether through affiliate marketing, dropshipping, blogging or creating and selling digital products. This diversity allows you to explore different options for maximising your income.

Unlimited growth potential: Online, there's no limit to the income you can generate. With the right strategy and a lot of effort, you can increase your earnings considerably over time. These advantages make working online an attractive option for those looking to increase their income or create an alternative source of finance. By exploiting the opportunities offered by the internet, it is possible to achieve your financial goals while enjoying greater freedom and flexibility in your working life.

The different ways of making money online

There are a multitude of methods for generating income online, each offering unique opportunities and tailored to different entrepreneurial profiles. Here are some of the main ways to make money online:

Affiliate marketing: Affiliate marketing involves promoting the products or services of other companies and earning a commission on the sales generated by your promotional efforts. It's a popular method because it doesn't require you to create products or manage stocks.

Dropshipping: Dropshipping is a business model where you sell products without having to physically stock them. You place an order with the supplier only when you receive an order from your customer, which considerably reduces the initial costs.

Blogging: Blogs are a popular platform for generating income online. By publishing quality content and attracting a loyal following, you can monetise your blog through advertising, sponsored posts or the sale of digital products.

Selling digital products: Creating and selling digital products such as ebooks, online courses or software can be a lucrative source of online revenue. Once the product has been created, you can sell it to an unlimited number of customers without having to bear the costs associated with physical production.

Freelance: Working as a freelancer on specialist platforms is another way of earning a living online. Whether you're a copywriter, graphic designer, web developer or consultant, there's a growing demand for freelance services in a variety of fields.

These different methods offer online entrepreneurs the opportunity to explore various sources of income and find the one that best suits their skills and financial goals. By combining several strategies or focusing on a single method, it is possible to create a profitable and sustainable business on the Internet.

The skills and resources needed to succeed

Generating revenue online requires a specific set of skills and resources to succeed in this competitive field. Here are some key elements to consider:

Technical skills: To succeed online, it's essential to master the digital tools and platforms used to generate revenue. Skills such as website design, SEO, social network management and content writing are essential if you are to stand out in a digital environment.

Marketing skills: Understanding the principles of online marketing is crucial to attracting a target audience and converting visitors into paying customers. Knowledge of advertising strategies, personal branding and data analysis can make the difference between the success and failure of an online business.

Financial resources: While some methods of generating income online require little initial investment, others may require more substantial financial resources. It is important to assess your financial capacity and plan an appropriate budget for developing your online business.

Networking and collaboration: In the digital world, networking with other online entrepreneurs can be a valuable source of opportunities and support. Collaborating with partners or influencers can also help increase your visibility and credibility on the internet. To succeed in online revenue generation, it is essential to develop a diverse set of technical, marketing and interpersonal skills. By combining these skills with well-managed financial resources and a strong network, entrepreneurs can maximise their chances of success in this dynamic digital world.

References:

https://www.lesaffaires.com/blogues/stephanie-leroux/gagner-sa-vie-sur-internet-les- cles-du-succes/611013

https://www.blogdumoderateur.com/reussir-business-en-ligne/

https://www.journaldunet.com/web-tech/dictionnaire-du-webmastering/1209341-passive-income-definition-and-examples/:~:text=A%20passive%20income%20is%20a,of%20fa%C3%A7on%20r%C3

2. AFFILIATE MARKETING

Understanding affiliate marketing and how it works

Affiliate marketing is a popular method of generating income online that involves promoting the products or services of other companies. The essence of affiliate marketing is that affiliates receive a commission for every sale or action generated through their promotional efforts. This approach allows affiliates to earn money without having to create or manage products, making it an attractive option for many online entrepreneurs. Affiliate marketing works on the basis of a partnership between the advertiser (the company offering the product or service) and the affiliate (the promoter). When an affiliate decides to promote a specific product, they receive a unique link, called an affiliate link, which enables them to track the sales and actions generated by their promotion. Each time a user clicks on this link and makes a purchase or performs a desired action, the affiliate earns a pre-determined commission. To be successful in affiliate marketing, it is essential for affiliates to choose products or services that are relevant to their target audience. In-depth knowledge of their audience and its needs is crucial to creating persuasive and effective content. In addition, affiliates should use various promotional channels such as blogs, social networks, newsletters or even paid advertising to maximise their visibility and increase their chances of conversion.In addition, transparency and ethics are key elements of affiliate marketing. Affiliates must clearly disclose their relationship with the advertiser in order to build trust with their audience. By respecting these fundamental principles and implementing effective strategies, affiliates can take full advantage of the lucrative potential of affiliate marketing while offering added value to their followers.

Find the best affiliation programmes to maximise your earnings

A crucial step in affiliate marketing is to find the programmes that offer the best earning opportunities. Here are some tips for choosing the best affiliate programmes:

In-depth research: Take the time to research and analyse different affiliation programmes in your niche. Compare the commissions offered, the payment terms, the reputation of the advertiser and the quality of the products or services on offer.

Matching your audience: Choose programmes that match the interests and needs of your target audience. Opt for products or services that will arouse the interest of your followers and increase your chances of conversion.

Advertiser reputation: Working with reliable, well-established advertisers can guarantee timely payments and a fruitful collaboration. Seek advice about the advertiser before committing to an affiliation programme.

Tools and support: Make sure the affiliate programme offers effective marketing tools such as banners, tracked links and promotional content. Good customer support is also essential to answer your questions and help you optimise your campaigns.

Earnings potential: Evaluate the earnings potential offered by each programme in terms of commission rate, expected sales volume and average amount per transaction. Choose programmes that offer a balance between profitability and feasibility. By following these tips, you'll be able to identify the best affiliation programmes to maximise your earnings. Don't forget that quality is more important than quantity. It's better to promote a few relevant products or services successfully than to spread your efforts over a multitude of low-performing offers.

Use effective strategies to promote products and generate sales

Once you have selected the best affiliate programmes, it is essential to use effective strategies to promote the products and increase your chances of generating sales. Here are a few tips to maximise your success as an affiliate:

Create quality content: Creating relevant and engaging content is essential to attracting the attention of your audience. Whether it's through blog articles, videos, podcasts or posts on social networks, make sure you provide informative content that highlights the benefits of the product you're promoting.

Use e-mail marketing: E-mail marketing is still one of the most effective ways of promoting affiliate products. Create a list of qualified subscribers and send them regular personalised newsletters with special offers and product recommendations.

Optimise referencing: Make sure your content is well referenced on search engines to attract organic traffic to your affiliate links. Use relevant keywords, create quality backlinks and optimise the structure of your website to improve your online visibility.

Collaborate with other influencers: Partnering with other influencers in your niche can help you extend your reach and reach a wider audience. By working together on promotional campaigns or sharing your content with each other, you can benefit from their credibility and already established audience.

Track and analyse your performance: Use analysis tools to track your performance in terms of clicks, conversions and revenue generated. Identify what works best for you and adjust your strategies accordingly to maximise your results.

By implementing these effective strategies, you will be able to promote affiliate products successfully and increase your chances of generating profitable sales. Constant engagement with your audience, continuous optimisation of your marketing efforts and intelligent collaboration with other key players are all key to success in affiliate marketing.

References:

https://www.blogdumoderateur.com/strategies-marketing-affiliation/https://www.webmarketing-conseil.fr/comment-promouvoir-produits-affiliation/
https://www.markentive.fr/blog/marketing-daffiliation-strategies-reussir/

3. DROPSHIPPING

3.1 What is dropshipping and how does it work?

Dropshipping is an increasingly popular business model that allows entrepreneurs to sell products without having to manage inventory or shipping. Unlike traditional e-commerce, where the seller must purchase and stock the products they sell, dropshipping involves the supplier shipping the products directly to the end customer on behalf of the seller.

Dropshipping works in a relatively simple way. The entrepreneur sets up an online shop to sell products supplied by wholesalers or manufacturers. When a customer places an order on the online shop, the seller forwards the order to the supplier, who then dispatches the product directly to the customer. The seller never physically handles the products, which considerably reduces the costs associated with inventory management and shipping.

A key aspect of dropshipping is the profit margin achieved by the seller. By setting a higher selling price than the purchase price agreed with the supplier, the seller can generate profits without having to invest in initial stock. However, it is essential to strike a balance between setting an attractive price for customers and achieving sufficient profit margins to keep the business profitable.

In addition, the success of dropshipping depends on selecting good suppliers and profitable products. Working with reliable partners who offer consistent quality and fast delivery times is crucial to ensuring customer satisfaction. In addition, choosing products that are popular and in demand by your target audience can increase your chances of success with this business model. In short, dropshipping offers entrepreneurs a unique opportunity to create an online business without the traditional logistical constraints. By understanding how this business model works and putting in place an effective strategy based on solid partnerships and a judicious selection of products, it is possible to take full advantage of dropshipping's lucrative potential.

3.2 Find the best suppliers and products to start your dropshipping business

When you launch your dropshipping business, finding the right suppliers and products is essential to the success of your online business. Selecting the right partners can have a significant impact on product quality, customer satisfaction and the overall profitability of your business. To find the best suppliers, it is advisable to carry out thorough research and evaluate several key criteria. Make sure your potential suppliers offer consistent product quality, fast shipping times and good customer service. You can consult online platforms specialising in dropshipping to discover new suppliers or contact manufacturers directly to establish solid partnerships. When it comes to choosing products, it's important to select items that are popular and in demand with your target audience. Analyse market trends, identify unmet needs and offer a varied range of attractive products to attract a wide range of potential customers. You should also make sure that you set competitive prices while preserving your profit margins to ensure the financial viability of your business. Another effective strategy is to test different suppliers and products before making final decisions. Launch pilot campaigns, analyse the performance of each product and assess the responsiveness and reliability of your suppliers in real-life situations. This approach will enable you to optimise your product catalogue and establish lasting relationships with reliable partners.In conclusion, finding the best suppliers and products to start your dropshipping business takes time, research and a strategic approach. By investing in the careful selection of your trading partners and offering an attractive range of profitable products, you can position your business for success in the competitive world of e-commerce.

3.3 Set up an effective online shop and optimise sales

Once you've found the best suppliers and products for your dropshipping business, it's essential to set up an effective online shop to maximise your sales. Good website design and a solid marketing strategy can mean the difference between success and failure for your business.

To start with, make sure your website is user-friendly, intuitive and professional. Choose an attractive design that highlights your products, makes it easy for customers to navigate and encourages impulse buying. Make sure your online shop is optimised for mobile devices, as more and more shoppers are making purchases on smartphones and tablets.

Next, develop a comprehensive marketing strategy to attract traffic to your website. Use techniques such as search engine optimisation (SEO), paid advertising (Google Ads, Facebook Ads), e-mail marketing and social networks to promote your products to a wide audience. Regularly analyse the performance of your marketing campaigns to adjust your strategy and maximise your return on investment.

Once you've attracted visitors to your website, make sure you optimise the buying process to increase your conversion rates. Simplify the ordering process, offer secure payment options and provide responsive customer service to reassure potential customers. Use web analysis tools to track user behaviour on your site and identify areas for improvement. Finally, don't forget the importance of after-sales service in retaining existing customers and encouraging positive recommendations. Offer quality customer support, deal quickly with any returns or problems customers encounter and constantly seek to improve the overall shopping experience on your online shop.

By combining a well-designed online shop with an effective marketing strategy and exceptional customer service, you can maximise your dropshipping sales and build a successful e-commerce business.

References:

https://www.oberlo.fr/blog/strategie-marketing-dropshipping

https://www.shopify.fr/guides/dropshipping

https://www.ecommerce-nation.fr/optimiser-votre-boutique-en-ligne-pour-le- dropshipping/

4. CREATING PROFITABLE CONTENT

4.1 Identify the types of content that generate revenue at .

Identifying profitable content types is essential for online content creators looking to maximise their revenues. Different content formats can be monetised in different ways, and understanding which types of content are most profitable in a given context is crucial.

Sponsored videos are one of the most lucrative types of content for many creators. Partnerships with brands to promote their products or services in videos can generate significant revenue through paid collaborations. Similarly, sponsored articles offer a similar opportunity for bloggers and influencers to get paid to write about specific brands or products.

Social media posts can also be an important source of online revenue. Influencers with a strong presence on platforms such as Instagram, TikTok or YouTube can work with brands to create sponsored content or promote products to their audience. These paid partnerships can be extremely profitable for creators with a committed subscriber base.

In addition, the creation and sale of digital products such as ebooks, online courses or graphic templates can provide a stable source of online revenue. Talented creators can monetise their expertise by offering exclusive content to an audience willing to pay for access to these specialist resources.

Finally, affiliate marketing is another popular strategy for generating online revenue through content. By recommending third-party products or services via affiliate links, creators can earn commission on every sale made as a result of their recommendation. This approach can be particularly lucrative if the creator has a loyal and engaged audience ready to follow their recommendations.In conclusion, identifying the types of content that generate revenue online requires a thorough understanding of the market and the target audience. By choosing wisely from the different options available and developing a strategy tailored to their area of expertise, a creator can fully exploit the financial potential offered by creating profitable content on the internet.

4.2 Create quality content that attracts your target audience

Creating quality content is essential to attracting and retaining a target audience. Understanding your audience's needs, interests and preferences is crucial to producing relevant and engaging content.

One effective approach is to carry out an in-depth analysis of your audience to identify the subjects that generate the most interest. By using social media analysis tools or surveys, you can gather valuable data on your audience's preferences and adapt your content accordingly.

In addition, diversifying the content format can help attract a wide range of audiences. In addition to written articles, consider integrating videos, infographics, podcasts or even webinars to offer a varied experience to your subscribers.

Another important aspect is the regularity with which content is published. By maintaining a regular and predictable cadence, you can build loyalty among your audience by providing them with a constant flow of new information and strengthening their trust in your brand.

Finally, don't forget the importance of interaction with your audience. Respond to comments, ask questions to encourage engagement and create a sense of community around your content. This will not only increase the loyalty of your audience, but also attract new subscribers through positive word-of-mouth. In conclusion, creating quality content that appeals to your target audience requires an in-depth understanding of their needs and preferences. By adapting your editorial strategy according to your audience's feedback, and by encouraging interaction and engagement, you can maximise the impact of your content and increase its profitability over the long term.

4.3 Monetise content through advertising, partnerships and digital products

When it comes to monetising your content, there are a number of effective strategies that can help you generate revenue while offering added value to your audience. Advertising, partnerships and digital products are popular ways of monetising your content.

Advertising is one of the most common ways of generating revenue from your content. You can embed advertisements on your website, videos or podcasts to reach a wide audience and earn money based on the number of views or clicks. It's essential to choose advertisers that are relevant to your audience in order to maximise your earnings and keep your subscribers engaged.

Partnerships with other brands or influencers can also be an interesting source of revenue. By collaborating with companies that share your values, you can create sponsored content or cross-promotions that benefit both your audience and your partners. Make sure these collaborations are transparent and genuine to maintain the trust of your audience.

Finally, creating and selling digital products can be another sustainable source of revenue. Whether it's ebooks, online courses, digital tools or even premium subscriptions, offering exclusive, high value-added content can encourage your audience to invest in your products. Make sure you promote these products strategically within your content to maximise their visibility and appeal.

By judiciously combining advertising, partnerships and digital products, you can diversify your sources of revenue while offering enriching and relevant content to your target audience. This proactive approach can help you not only to make your content profitable but also to strengthen the loyalty of your subscribers over the long term.

References:

https://www.blogdumoderateur.com/monetiser-contenu-digital/

https://www.lesechos.fr/idees-debats/cercle/opinion-comment-monetiser-son-contenu-sur-internet-1313666

https://www.journaldunet.com/web-tech/dictionnaire-du-webmastering/1445724-monetisation-definition-and-strategies-for-making-money-with-a-website/

5. EFFICIENT MANAGEMENT OF TIME AND RESOURCES

5.1 Plan your online activities to maximise your productivity

When it comes to managing time and resources effectively online, activity planning plays a crucial role in maximising productivity. By establishing a clear, structured schedule, individuals can organise their tasks strategically to maximise their efficiency.

The first step is to identify the priorities and objectives to be achieved. By clearly defining what needs to be done, it becomes easier to allocate time and resources appropriately. This avoids procrastination and allows you to concentrate on the tasks that are essential to progress towards your goals. Next, it's important to draw up a realistic timetable, taking into account personal and professional constraints. By allocating specific time slots to each activity, it becomes easier to maintain discipline and regularity in carrying out the planned tasks.

Using online time management tools can also be beneficial for effective planning. Applications such as Trello, Asana or Google Calendar offer features for organising tasks, setting deadlines and tracking the progress of projects in real time.

Finally, building breaks and recovery time into your schedule is essential to avoid burnout and maintain optimum levels of productivity. Taking the time to rest and recharge can improve concentration and creativity when you return to work.

In conclusion, planning your online activities rigorously and methodically is a key factor in maximising your productivity. By adopting a proactive approach to organising your time and using the right tools, you can optimise the use of available resources to successfully achieve your objectives.

5.2 Use tools and techniques to optimise your time and your resources

When it comes to optimising your time and resources, using the right tools and techniques can make it much easier to manage your activities effectively. By incorporating these elements into your planning, you can maximise productivity and achieve your objectives more efficiently.

Using time management applications: Applications such as Trello, Asana, Todoist or Google Calendar offer a host of features for organising tasks, setting deadlines, sharing team projects and tracking progress in real time. These tools provide a better overview of the activities to be carried out and help you prioritise tasks according to their importance and urgency.

Time management techniques: The Pomodoro technique, based on intervals of concentrated work followed by short breaks, can help maintain concentration while avoiding mental fatigue. Similarly, the Eisenhower method, which consists of classifying tasks according to their urgency and importance, helps you to organise your time better by concentrating on essential activities.

Outsourcing non-priority tasks: To make the most of your time, it's sometimes a good idea to outsource certain non-essential tasks. Using a virtual assistant or delegating responsibilities can free up time to focus on the key activities that need attention.

These tools and techniques are not only useful for managing time, but also for optimising the use of available resources. By combining rigorous planning with the appropriate integration of digital tools and proven methods, it is possible to significantly improve efficiency in the accomplishment of daily tasks.

Avoid the common pitfalls of managing time and resources online

When it comes to effectively managing your time and resources online, it's crucial to avoid certain common pitfalls that can hamper productivity and success. By identifying these potential obstacles, you can bypass them and significantly improve your time and resource management.

Information overload: One of the main pitfalls online is the overabundance of information available, which can lead to time being wasted navigating between different sources without actually completing important tasks. It is essential to define clear objectives and limit the consumption of irrelevant information in order to stay focused on priority tasks.

Digital distractions: Online distractions such as incessant social network notifications, non-urgent emails or browsing unprofessional websites can significantly affect time management. It is advisable to set aside dedicated periods without interruptions so that you can concentrate fully on important tasks.

Misuse of digital tools: Although digital tools can be extremely useful for optimising time management, misusing them can also be a pitfall. It's essential to choose the right applications for your specific needs and not be overwhelmed by a multitude of useless tools that complicate rather than help.

By avoiding these common pitfalls of online time and resource management, you can maximise your efficiency and productivity. By remaining aware of these potential obstacles and adopting strategies to get around them, it's easier to achieve your professional goals while maintaining a healthy balance between your personal and professional life.

References:

Article on the management of time and of resources atonline-
www.exemple.com/gestion-temps-en-ligne

Guide guide for avoid the distractions digita-
www.exemple.com/distractions-numeriques

Book on optimisation from the productivity with the tools digital tools - www.exemple.com/productivite-outils-numeriques

6. PERSEVERANCE AND CREATIVITY TO SUCCEED ONLINE

6.1 Cultivate a success mentality and overcome obstacles

Online success depends not only on technical skills, but also on a positive and perseverant mindset. Cultivating a success mindset means believing in your abilities, being resilient in the face of setbacks and staying motivated despite the obstacles you encounter.

To overcome obstacles, it's essential to set clear, achievable goals. Having a clear vision of what you want to achieve makes it easier to stay focused and determined. What's more, learning to turn setbacks into learning opportunities means you can bounce back more quickly and move towards success.

Perseverance plays a crucial role in achieving online goals. In the face of challenges and setbacks, it's important to stay motivated and keep moving forward despite the difficulties. The ability to persist in your efforts, to adapt to change and to meet challenges with determination are essential qualities for success online.

In addition, it is essential to develop a proactive attitude in the face of obstacles. Rather than being discouraged by the difficulties encountered, it is necessary to adopt a constructive approach by seeking alternative solutions and remaining open to the changes needed to progress towards your objectives.

In conclusion, cultivating a success mindset and overcoming

obstacles are key to online success. By adopting a positive, persevering and proactive attitude, it becomes possible to face challenges with confidence and determination, paving the way to professional success on the Internet.

6.2 Find creative solutions to stand out in a competitive market

In a saturated and competitive online environment, it is essential to find creative solutions to stand out from the crowd and attract the attention of potential customers. Creativity can be a major asset for companies seeking to position themselves uniquely in the marketplace.

An innovative approach can take many forms, from designing original products to implementing innovative marketing campaigns and creating an exceptional customer experience. By pushing traditional boundaries and thinking outside the box, a company can captivate its target audience and differentiate itself from its competitors.

Creativity is not just limited to the field of design or marketing; it can also extend to the way a company approaches its internal processes. By adopting innovative ways of working, such as flexible teleworking, interdisciplinary collaboration or the integration of disruptive technologies, a company can not only improve its operational efficiency but also strengthen its market position.

Creativity can also be seen in the way a company communicates with its audience. By using social networks in original ways, launching viral campaigns or offering engaging and entertaining content, a company can arouse the interest and commitment of its online community.

In conclusion, finding creative solutions to stand out in a competitive market is essential for online success. By cultivating a spirit of innovation and constantly exploring new ideas and approaches, a business can not only survive in a competitive environment but also prosper and grow sustainably on the internet.

6.3 Adapt to change and seize opportunities to continue generating revenue

The ability to adapt to rapid changes in the online market is crucial to maintaining the viability of a business and continuing to generate revenue. Companies that remain set in their ways risk being overtaken by the competition and losing market share. It is therefore essential to remain agile and flexible in order to seize opportunities as they arise. An effective strategy for adapting to change is to keep a close eye on market trends, consumer behaviour and technological developments. By staying constantly informed, a company can anticipate future changes and adjust its strategy accordingly. For example, if a new social media platform gains in popularity, a company must be prepared to invest time and resources in it to reach a new audience. In addition, it is important to encourage a culture of innovation within the company so that employees are encouraged to come up with innovative ideas in response to changing market challenges. Creativity and collaboration can lead to unique solutions that allow the company to stand out and remain relevant.Finally, seizing opportunities to continue generating revenue also means being proactive in seeking out new sources of income. This may involve developing new products or services, exploring strategic partnerships or even diversifying online sales channels. By being constantly on the lookout for expansion opportunities, a company can ensure its continued growth in the digital marketplace.In conclusion, adapting to change and seizing opportunities are key to maintaining the competitiveness and profitability of an online business. By adopting a proactive approach and fostering innovation, a business can not only survive in a dynamic environment but also prosper in the long term.

References:

Smith, J. (2020). How to adapt to rapid changes in the online marketplace. Harvard Business Review.

Dupont, A. (2019). The importance of innovation to capture revenue opportunities. Journal of Business Strategy.

Gagnon, C. et al. (2018). Growth strategies for online businesses.International journal of management and economics.

BOOK SUMMARY

You can work anytime, anywhere, making it easy to balance your professional and personal life. You can start with little or no money and gradually build up your business. You can reach customers all over the world. This diversity allows you to explore different options to maximise your income.These advantages make working online an attractive option for those looking to increase their income or create an alternative source of finance. By exploiting the opportunities offered by the internet, it is possible to achieve your financial goals while enjoying greater freedom and flexibility in your working life. There are a multitude of methods for generating income online, each offering unique opportunities and tailored to different entrepreneurial profiles.

The different ways of making money online

It's a popular method because it doesn't require you to create products or manage stocks. By publishing quality content and attracting a loyal following, you can monetise your blog through advertising, sponsored posts or the sale of digital products. Once the product has been created, you can sell it to an unlimited number of customers without having to bear the costs associated with physical production. Whether you're Whether you're a copywriter, graphic designer, web developer or consultant, there's a growing demand for freelance services in a variety of fields.These different methods offer online entrepreneurs the opportunity to explore various sources of income and find the one that best suits their skills and financial goals. By combining several strategies or focusing on a single method, it is possible to create a profitable and sustainable online business. Generating income online requires a specific set of skills and resources to succeed in this competitive field.

The skills and resources needed to succeed

Skills such as website design, SEO, social network management and content writing are essential if you are to stand out in a digital environment. Knowledge of advertising strategies, personal branding and data analysis can make the difference between the success and failure of an online business. It is important to assess your financial capabilities and plan an appropriate budget for developing your online business. Working with partners or influencers can also help to increase your visibility and credibility on the Internet.To succeed in online revenue generation, it is essential to develop a diverse set of technical, marketing and interpersonal skills. By combining these skills with well-managed financial resources and a strong network, entrepreneurs can maximise their chances of success in this dynamic digital world.

Find the best affiliation programmes to maximise your earnings

Compare the commissions offered, the payment terms, the advertiser's reputation and the quality of the products or services on offer. Opt for products or services that will arouse the interest of your followers and increase your chances of conversion. Seek out reviews of the advertiser before committing to an affiliation programme. Good customer support is also essential to answer your questions and help you optimise your campaigns.By following these tips, you'll be able to identify the best affiliation programmes to maximise your earnings. Remember that quality is more important than quantity, so it's better to promote a few relevant products or services successfully than to spread your efforts over a multitude of low-performing offers. Once you have selected the best affiliation programmes, it is essential to use effective strategies to promote the products and increase your chances of generating sales.

Use effective strategies to promote products and generate sales

Whether through blog articles, videos, podcasts or posts on social networks, make sure you provide informative content that highlights the benefits of the product you are promoting. Use relevant keywords, create quality backlinks and optimise the structure of your website to improve your online visibility. By working together on promotional campaigns or sharing your content, you can benefit from their credibility and their established audience. Identify what works best for you and adjust your strategies accordingly to maximise your results.

By implementing these effective strategies, you will be able to promote affiliate products successfully and increase your chances of generating sales. profitable. Constant engagement with your audience, continuous optimisation of your marketing efforts and intelligent collaboration with other key players are all key to success in affiliate marketing. Dropshipping is an increasingly popular business model that allows entrepreneurs to sell products without having to manage inventory or shipping. Unlike traditional e-commerce, where the seller must purchase and store the products they sell, dropshipping involves the supplier shipping the products directly to the end customer on behalf of the seller.

Dropshipping works in a relatively simple way. The entrepreneur sets up an online shop to sell products supplied by wholesalers or manufacturers. When a customer places an order on the online shop, the seller forwards the order to the supplier, who then dispatches the product directly to the customer. A key aspect of dropshipping is the profit margin achieved by the seller. In addition, the success of dropshipping depends on the selection of good suppliers and profitable products. In short, dropshipping offers entrepreneurs a unique opportunity to create an online business without the traditional logistical constraints. By understanding how this business model works and putting in place an effective strategy based on solid partnerships and a judicious selection of products, it is possible to take full advantage of dropshipping's lucrative potential.

Find the best suppliers and products to start your dropshipping business

When you launch your dropshipping business, finding the right suppliers and products is essential to the success of your online business. You can consult online platforms specialising in dropshipping to discover new suppliers or contact manufacturers directly to establish strong partnerships. When it comes to choosing products, it's important to select items that are popular and in demand with your target audience. In conclusion, finding the best suppliers and products to start your dropshipping business takes time, research and a strategic approach. Once you've found the best suppliers and products for your dropshipping business, it's essential to set up an effective online shop to maximise your sales. Good website design and a solid marketing strategy can mean the difference between success and failure for your business. Make sure your online shop is optimised for mobile devices, as more and more shoppers are making purchases on smartphones and tablets. Use techniques such as search engine optimisation, paid advertising, e-mail marketing and social networks to promote your products to a wide audience.Offer quality customer support, deal quickly with customer returns or problems and constantly strive to improve the overall shopping experience on your online shop. By combining a well-designed online shop with an effective marketing strategy and exceptional customer service, you can maximise your dropshipping sales and build a successful e-commerce business. Identifying profitable content types is essential for online content creators looking to maximise their revenue. Different content formats can be monetised in different ways, and understanding which types of content are most profitable in a given context is crucial. Partnerships with brands to promote their products or services in videos can generate significant revenue through paid collaborations. Publications on social networks can also be a major source of revenue by online. Instagram, TikTok or YouTube can work with brands to create sponsored content or promote products to their audience. These paid partnerships can be extremely profitable for creators with a committed subscriber base. In addition, the creation and sale of digital products such as ebooks, online courses or graphic templates can provide a stable source of online revenue. Talented creators can monetise their expertise by offering exclusive content to an audience willing to pay for access to these specialist resources. Finally, affiliate marketing is another popular strategy for generating online revenue through content. By recommending third-party products or services via affiliate links, creators can earn commission on every sale made as a result of their recommendation. This approach can be particularly lucrative if the creator has a loyal and committed audience ready to follow their recommendations. In conclusion, identifying the types of content that generate revenue online requires a thorough understanding of the market and the target audience. Creating quality content is the key to attracting and retaining a target audience. To do this, it is crucial to understand the needs, interests and preferences of your audience in order to produce relevant and engaging content. One effective approach is to carry out an in-depth analysis of your audience to identify the subjects that generate the most interest. By using social media analysis tools or surveys, you can gather valuable data on your audience's preferences and adapt your content accordingly. In addition, diversifying the content format can help to attract a wide range of audiences. By maintaining a regular, predictable cadence, you can build audience loyalty by providing them with a constant stream of new information and boosting their trust in your brand. Finally, don't forget the importance of interaction with your audience. In conclusion, creating quality content that appeals to your target audience requires a thorough understanding of their needs and preferences. By adapting your editorial strategy according to your audience's feedback, and by encouraging interaction and engagement, you can maximise the impact of your content and increase its profitability over the long term.

Monetising content through advertising, partnerships and digital products

When it comes to monetising your content, there are several effective strategies that can help you generate revenue while offering added value to your audience. You can embed advertisements on your website, videos or podcasts to reach a wide audience and get paid based on the number of views or clicks. It is essential to choose advertisers that are relevant to your audience in order to maximise your earnings and keep your subscribers engaged. Partnerships with other brands or influencers can also be an interesting source of income. By collaborating with like-minded companies, you can create sponsored content or cross-promotions that benefit both your audience and your partners. Make sure these collaborations are transparent and authentic to maintain the trust of your audience. Finally, creating and selling digital products can be another sustainable source of income. Whether it's ebooks, online courses, digital tools or even subscriptions premium, offering exclusive content with high added value can encourage your audience to invest in your products. By judiciously combining advertising, partnerships and digital products, you can diversify your sources of revenue while offering enriching and relevant content to your target audience. When it comes to managing time and resources effectively online, activity planning plays a crucial role in maximising productivity. By establishing a clear and structured calendar, individuals can organise their tasks to optimise their efficiency. Using online time management tools can also be beneficial for effective planning. In conclusion, planning your online activities rigorously and methodically is a key factor in maximising your productivity.

Use tools and techniques to optimise time and resources

When it comes to optimising your time and resources, using the right tools and techniques can make it much easier to manage your activities effectively.

Using time management applications: Applications such as

Trello, Asana, Todoist and Google Calendar offer a host of features for organising tasks, setting deadlines, sharing projects as a team and tracking progress in real time. Similarly, the Eisenhower method, which consists of classifying tasks according to their urgency and importance, helps you to better organise your schedule by focusing on essential activities. Using a virtual assistant or delegating responsibilities can free up time to focus on the key activities that need attention. These tools and techniques are not only useful for managing time, but also for optimising the use of available resources. When it comes to effectively managing your time and resources online, it's crucial to avoid certain common pitfalls that can hamper productivity and success. By identifying these potential obstacles, it is possible to bypass them and significantly improve time and resource management. It is essential to define clear objectives and limit the consumption of irrelevant information in order to stay focused on priority tasks. It is advisable to set up dedicated periods without interruptions so that you can concentrate fully on the important tasks. It's essential to choose the right applications for your specific needs and not be overwhelmed by a multitude of useless tools that complicate rather than help. By avoiding these common pitfalls of online time and resource management, you can maximise your efficiency and productivity. Book productivity optimisation www.exemple.com/productivite-outils-numeriques with tools.

Perseverance and creativity for success in

Success online depends not only on technical skills, but also on a positive and perseverant mindset. Setting clear, achievable goals is the key to overcoming obstacles. Perseverance plays a crucial role in achieving online goals. The ability to persist in your efforts, to adapt to change and to meet challenges with determination are essential qualities for success online. Rather than being discouraged by the difficulties encountered, you need to adopt a constructive approach by looking for alternative solutions and remaining open to the changes needed to progress towards your goals. In conclusion, cultivating a success mentality and overcoming obstacles are key to online success.

Finding creative solutions to stand out in a competitive market

In a saturated and competitive online environment, it's essential to find creative ways of standing out and attracting the attention of potential customers. By using social networks in original ways, launching viral campaigns or offering engaging and entertaining content, a company can arouse the interest and commitment of its online community. In conclusion, finding creative solutions to stand out in a competitive market is essential to online success. By cultivating a spirit of innovation and constantly exploring new ideas and approaches, a business can not only survive in a competitive environment but also prosper and grow sustainably online.

Adapting to change and seizing opportunities to continue generating revenue

The ability to adapt to rapid changes in the online market is crucial to maintaining the viability of a business and continuing to generate revenue. An effective strategy for adapting to change is to keep a close eye on market trends, consumer behaviour and technological developments. By staying constantly informed, a company can anticipate future changes and adjust its strategy accordingly. For example, if a new social media platform gains in popularity, a company must be prepared to invest time and resources to reach a new audience.In conclusion, adapting to change and seizing opportunities are key to maintaining the competitiveness and profitability of an online business. How to adapt to rapid changes in the online market. Growth strategies for online businesses. International journal of management and economics. How to make $1,000 a day online is an invaluable resource for those looking to generate income online effectively. The author explores in depth the strategies, tools and techniques needed to achieve this goal ambitious. Through an in-depth analysis of the online marketplace, this book offers a unique perspective on the lucrative opportunities that exist on the internet. Whether through affiliate marketing, dropshipping, content creation or other means, the author guides the reader through the essential steps to starting and developing a profitable online business. With its emphasis on perseverance, creativity and effective management of time and resources, "How to earn $1,000 a day on the Internet" offers a concrete action plan for those who want to transform their online presence into a stable and significant source of income.

How to make $1,000 a day online" is an invaluable resource for those looking to generate income online effectively. The author explores in depth the strategies, tools and techniques needed to achieve this ambitious goal.

Based on a systematic approach and in-depth research, the author presents valuable information and practical advice on how to maximise your earnings on the Internet. Case studies, expert testimonials and detailed analyses are used to illustrate the different methods available and help readers find the one that suits them best.

Through an in-depth analysis of the online marketplace, this book offers a unique perspective on the lucrative opportunities that exist on the internet. Whether through affiliate marketing, dropshipping, content creation or other means, the author guides the reader through the essential steps to starting and developing a profitable online business.

With its emphasis on perseverance, creativity and effective management of time and resources, "How to earn $1,000 a day on the Internet" offers a concrete action plan for those who want to transform their online presence into a stable and significant source of income.

This book is an essential guide for anyone who wants to succeed in today's digital economy. It offers not only practical knowledge but also an invitation to take your financial destiny into your own hands through the limitless possibilities offered by the internet.

yes

I want morebooks!

Buy your books fast and straightforward online - at one of world's fastest growing online book stores! Environmentally sound due to Print-on-Demand technologies.

Buy your books online at

www.morebooks.shop

Kaufen Sie Ihre Bücher schnell und unkompliziert online – auf einer der am schnellsten wachsenden Buchhandelsplattformen weltweit! Dank Print-On-Demand umwelt- und ressourcenschonend produzi ert.

Bücher schneller online kaufen

www.morebooks.shop

info@omniscriptum.com
www.omniscriptum.com

Printed by Books on Demand GmbH, Norderstedt / Germany